A Penguin Year

A Penguin Year

Written and Illustrated by
Susan Bonners

A Young Yearling Book

Published by
Dell Publishing
a division of
Bantam Doubleday Dell Publishing
Group, Inc.
666 Fifth Avenue
New York, New York 10103

The trademark Yearling® is registered in
the U.S. Patent and Trademark Office.

ISBN: 0-440-40151-8

Reprinted by arrangement with
Delacorte Press

Printed in the United States of America

March 1989

10 9 8 7 6 5 4 3 2 1

To Jim Frenkel, who once made a suggestion

Adélie penguins live in the Antarctic. This is the region around the South Pole, the coldest part of the earth. Surrounded by the Antarctic Ocean, the continent is covered by ice all year long.

Only tiny mosslike plants grow under the ice. No people live in the Antarctic except scientists, but this land of ice and snow is home to millions of penguins and seals and seabirds. The Adélie penguin is a bird, too, but a very special kind of bird.

It is winter in the Antarctic. An hour ago, the sun rose. Now it is setting. The seawater is almost freezing.

From under the water, a bird leaps up and lands feet first on an ice floe. One after another, twenty more birds follow him.

They are Adélie penguins, and they are very much at home in this cold world. Each penguin has a layer of fat and an oily feather coat to keep it warm.

The penguins have plenty of food. They eat krill, little shrimplike creatures that swim by the millions in the sea around them. But soon it will be spring and time to leave the open sea.

In late September, spring comes to the Southern Hemisphere. The days grow longer. Millions of penguins begin to swim to the continent of Antarctica, returning to the places where they were hatched.

As they get closer to the continent, they find the ice floes frozen together. From here on, the penguins walk. Where the ice is smooth, they toboggan.

The penguins have no food once they leave the water. They will live on the fat they stored up during their winter in the sea.

Each flock marches in single file for miles. There are no landmarks to help them find their way, but they never get lost. They use the sun to guide them.

Two weeks later, one flock has reached some scattered stones. This is its rookery. Each year, these penguins make their nests and raise their young here.

The penguins are tired. They rest through the night.

The next morning, Brush-tail, a six-year-old male, stretches and yawns. He begins to search among the stones. At last he finds what he is looking for—the exact spot where his nest was last year.

He points his beak straight up and shakes his flippers, calling in a loud voice:

"Ark! A-a-ark!"

Scarred-wing, his mate last year, hears him. She, too, has remembered the old nesting place. Luckily, she has returned. During the winter, she was almost eaten by a leopard seal, which caught her by a flipper.

Scarred-wing stands a few feet away from Brush-tail at first. He bobs his head to her. She bows in return, shuffling sideways toward him. Bobbing their heads over and over, they come closer together.

Brush-tail lies down and scrapes the ground with his feet, marking the place for a new nest. When she is ready, Scarred-wing lies down there.

Scarred-wing allows Brush-tail to stand on her back so that they may touch at a spot just under their tails. They bring their heads together and touch beaks, too, while they mate. Then they stand up, waving their heads and calling noisily.

Penguins may look alike, but each penguin's voice is different. By calling back and forth, Brush-tail and Scarred-wing learn to recognize each other's voices again.

Piling up a mound of stones, they begin to build a nest. Some stones are frozen into the ice. By sitting on them, the penguins thaw them free.

But it is easier to steal stones from a neighbor's nest—if the neighbor does not notice. Round and round, the stones are plucked from one nest to another.

Meanwhile, thousands of penguins are marching into the rookery in lines many miles long. The ice turns to mud under so many feet.

Young birds nesting for the first time have to fight for places. The males hammer each other with flippers and beaks.

The cries and screeches of the penguins never stop.

At the edges of the rookery, the first skua gulls return to their nests. They are meat-eaters. They will watch for the first penguin eggs, and then, the chicks.

By early November, the rookery has settled down. More than a million birds have found places here. They have grouped themselves in many small neighborhoods. Brush-tail and Scarred-wing's neighborhood has about fifty nests in it.

Scarred-wing lays two eggs in the nest. By now, she is thin and her white front is muddy. She joins a small group of other females for a trip back to the ocean for food.

Brush-tail stays behind, sitting on the eggs to keep them warm.

In the spring sunshine, the ice around the continent has begun to melt. Scarred-wing has to walk only a few miles to reach the open water.

When the weary females see the water, they rush to the edge of the ice. They begin to chatter and chase one another playfully. Scarred-wing peers out over the water. A hungry leopard seal might be hiding there, waiting to catch a penguin.

When the water looks safe, she dives in. Immediately, the rest follow. In the icy water, they clean the mud off their feathers.

On land, a penguin's
walk is a clumsy waddle.
With its small flippers and
heavy body, it cannot take
off into the air. But, under
the water, a penguin can
fly.

Up and down, with powerful strokes, the flippers work like wings. Penguins use their feet to steer. The sleek bodies shoot through the water.

Like a fish, Scarred-wing darts one way, then another. Like a duck, she floats on the water, paddling with flippers and feet.

To go faster, Scarred-wing swims like a porpoise, leaping up for a quick breath whenever she needs one.

Soon the penguins are far out at sea.

Whales and seals of many kinds are also hunting the krill. Thousands of birds fly overhead, diving to the water for food.

After two weeks in the sea, Scarred-wing is fat again. It is time to return to the rookery. From now on, her trips to the sea will be only two or three days long.

On shore again, Scarred-wing picks her way carefully through the rookery to reach her nest. Penguins sitting on their eggs peck at her if she comes too close.

As she approaches her nest, Scarred-wing clucks softly to Brush-tail. He will not leave the nest until he recognizes her voice.

Without food for five weeks, Brush-tail has lost half his weight. Even so, before he leaves, he fetches a few stones to repair the nest. Then he goes for his turn at sea.

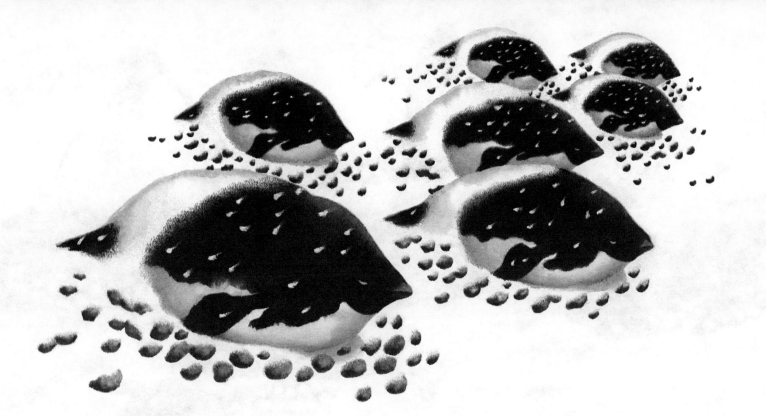

In the Antarctic, snowstorms may come at any time, even in the summer. After Brush-tail leaves, a few flakes fall, then more and more. The wind begins to howl across the rookery. Scarred-wing pulls her head close to her body. The heat of her breathing keeps an opening in the drift above her.

For more than a week, she remains in her chamber of ice until the sun melts it.

By early December, Brush-tail has returned from the sea, and Scarred-wing has gone for her second feeding trip.

The summer sun shines almost twenty-four hours a day. The air temperature is just below freezing, but this is warm for penguins. Brush-tail opens his beak and holds out his flippers to cool off.

The sun heats the ground. The snow melts. Some nests are in danger of flooding. The eggs will spoil if they sit in the cold water. The birds spend hours building their nests up higher with more stones.

Scarred-wing returns from the sea. Now that she and Brush-tail are fat again, they do not have to spend so much time catching krill. They have time to play.

While Brush-tail guards the eggs, Scarred-wing hops onto the ice floes that drift past the rookery and calls to the penguins on shore. Then she dives off and swims back for another ride.

Then, while **Scarred-wing** sits on the nest, **Brush-tail** climbs steep snow cliffs just to look around. Then he climbs down again.

At the beginning of the second week of December, there is a tapping sound in Scarred-wing's nest. The eggs are starting to crack. A tiny beak appears, then a head. At last, an exhausted chick frees itself from the shell.

Soon, it is peeping with hunger.

Scarred-wing has krill stored in a sac in her throat. When she hears her chick peeping, she brings this food up into her mouth. The chick reaches in for it.

The chicks have fluffy silvery-gray down. They keep their
heads tucked under Brush-tail and Scarred-wing. They
could not survive for even a few minutes without warmth.

When they are ten days old, the
down becomes brown and
woolly. The chicks begin to wave
their heads and peep when
Brush-tail and Scarred-wing
call. The chicks and their parents
learn one another's voices. Now
each of them will know the
others from the thousands of
penguins around them.

The tiny chicks are always hungry. When they are three weeks old, each chick eats three-and-a-half pounds of food a day, as much as it weighs.

Brush-tail and Scarred-wing are too busy to guard the nest now. Both must go to the sea every day to bring back enough food.

The chicks are left alone for the first time. Overhead, the skua gulls are circling. They are waiting to swoop down on eggs that roll from the nests or chicks that wander from their parents.

Skuas have hungry chicks to feed, too.

Sometimes, one skua will fight with a penguin while another grabs an egg or chick from the nest.

Often, eggs are knocked out of the nests when penguins fight with one another. Penguins ignore eggs that have rolled out of the nests. They chill quickly and will not hatch.

Skuas help clear the rookery of these spoiled eggs.

For protection from the skuas, the chicks in each neighborhood gather into a "crèche," which means "day nursery." Skuas are less likely to take a chick from such a large group. They look for strays.

As the skuas wheel slowly over the crèche, snow begins
to fall. A snowdrift could surround a single chick very
quickly. In the crèche, the chicks shield each other from
the snow.

While the flakes swirl around them, the chicks huddle
tightly together.

At last, Brush-tail comes back from the sea with food.
He goes to his nest and calls.

"A-a-ark!"

In the middle of the crèche, his hungry chicks hear him.
They push through the crowd of chicks and race to the nest.

Other chicks are so hungry that they rush over, too.
Brush-tail will not feed strangers. He pecks at them, but
they will not stop begging. At last, he runs away.

Soon, the strangers give up the chase. But Brush-tail's
chicks keep running after him until they are fed.

The chicks stay in the crèche for more than a month. By the time they are eight weeks old, they no longer have to fear the skuas. They are too big to be carried off. They are three-quarters grown. Waterproof feathers have replaced their fuzzy down.

The young birds wander back to their old nesting places. Only scattered stones are left.

Brush-tail and Scarred-wing feed their young for a little while longer. The time has come for the older birds to head for their winter home at sea. The young birds do not need them now. One day, Brush-tail and Scarred-wing leave the rookery and do not come back.

They swim far out to sea to fatten up on krill. Soon they will molt, shedding their worn-out feathers and growing new ones. While their new feathers are growing in, they will not be able to go into the water for food. They will stay on an ice floe.

The days are growing shorter. Most of the skua gulls have flown away. The young penguins run back and forth along the shore, exercising their flippers and calling to one another.

At first, they seem afraid to go into the water, but the pull of the sea is too strong. One by one, they splash into the waves.

The young penguins have never been in the water before. They cannot swim as fast as their parents. Some of them are taken by the leopard seals. The rest paddle to nearby ice floes and float out to sea. Those that reach the open water may go on to live for a dozen years or more.

Next year, when they return to the rookery, they will have black chins and white eye rings. They will weigh about eleven pounds and be about two feet tall.

In March, autumn comes to Antarctica. The last
penguins leave the rookery. They swim out to sea, where
they will join the whales and seals. A long winter of
playing and hunting krill lies ahead of them before spring
comes to Antarctica again and a new penguin year begins.